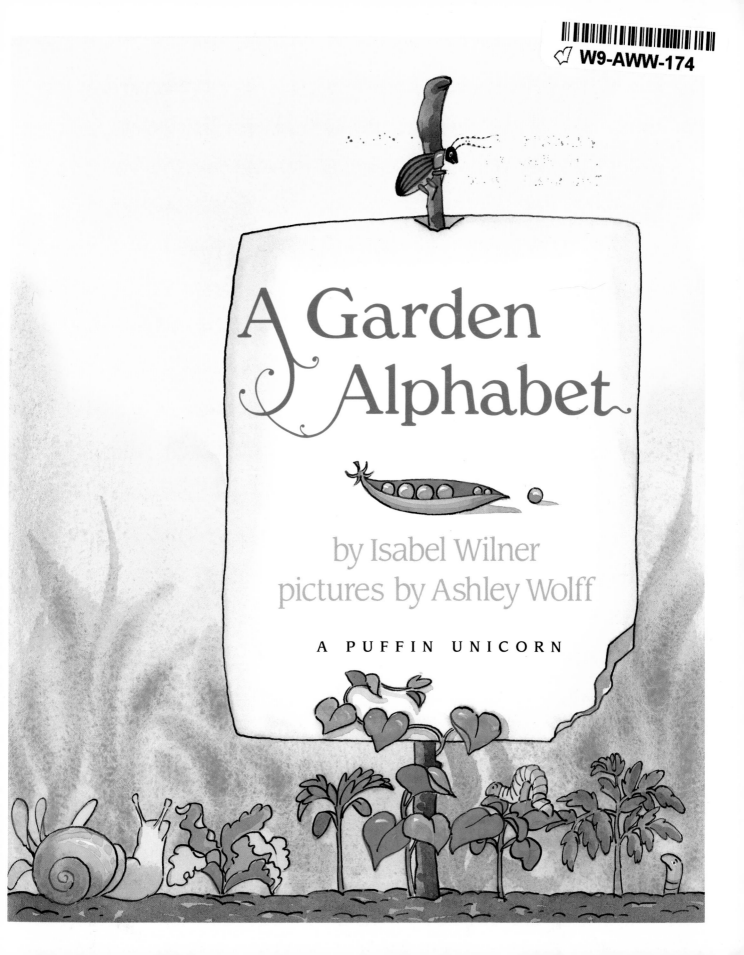

A Garden Alphabet

by Isabel Wilner
pictures by Ashley Wolff

A PUFFIN UNICORN

PUFFIN UNICORN BOOKS
Published by the Penguin Group • Penguin Books
USA Inc., 375 Hudson Street, New York, New York
10014, USA • Penguin Books Ltd, 27 Wrights Lane,
London W8 5TZ, England • Penguin Books Australia
Ltd, Ringwood, Victoria, Australia • Penguin Books
Canada Ltd, 10 Alcorn Avenue, Toronto, Ontario,
Canada M4V 3B2 • Penguin Books (N.Z.) Ltd, 182-
190 Wairau Road, Auckland 10, New Zealand
• Penguin Books Ltd, Registered Offices:
Harmondsworth, Middlesex, England

Text copyright © 1991 by Isabel Wilner • Illustrations
copyright © 1991 by Ashley Wolff • All rights reserved.
• Unicorn is a registered trademark of Dutton Children's
Books, a division of Penguin Books USA Inc. • Library
of Congress number 90-19619 • ISBN 0-14-055644-3 •
Published in the United States by Dutton Children's Books,
a division of Penguin Books USA Inc. • Designed by
Barbara Powderly • Printed in Hong Kong • First Puffin
Unicorn Edition 1995 • 10 9 8 7 6 5 4 3 2 1

A Garden Alphabet is also available in hardcover from
Dutton Children's Books.

For two gardening friends,
Ella Bramblett and Maud Broyles
—I.W.

For Pumpkin, of course
—A.W.

Aa is for April—warm rains at hand.
Bees begin buzzing. Gardens get planned.

Bb is for boundary, the edge of the plot.
Inside is garden. Outside is not.

Cc is for catalog,
a gardener's guide.
Some plants are favorites,
some not yet tried.

BEET

CARROT

BEAN

D

Dd is for dirt.
Down go the roots.
When a seed sprouts,
up come the shoots.

Ee is for earthworms.
They live where seeds sprout
And loosen the soil
as they burrow about.

Ff is for frog, a gardener's friend.
For unwelcome insects, his tongue snaps The End.

Gg is for grasshopper, a gardener's foe,
Eager to eat what's beginning to grow.

Hh is for hoe—
what the gardener needs
To turn over dirt and to
root out the weeds.

Ii is for inchworm
whose measuring walk
Marks the width of a leaf
and the length of a stalk.

Jj is for June—
warm days, sunny hours
When butterflies flutter by,
buttering flowers.

Kk is for kale, with leaves dark and wrinkled.
Its edges are crumpled, curly, and crinkled.

Ll is for lettuce, a leafy sphere molded—
Green layer upon layer, all carefully folded.

Mm is for munch—what the rabbits will do
If they find that you've left them a carrot or two.

Nn's for nasturtium,
a flower so bright,
Blazing red, orange, yellow—
like flashes of light.

Oo is for onion. When it's tender and small,
You can pull it right up and eat
bulb, stalk, and all.

P is for peas resting plump in a line
In a little green hammock
that grows on a vine.

Qq is for questions. To pick? To let grow?
A book and a look and a gardener will know.

Rr is for rabbits, back here once more.
Do they think they're the ones that the garden is for?

Ss is for snail slipping over the loam,
Taking its time, taking its home.

Tt's for tomato—
ripe, juicy, and fat.
No garden can offer
better than that!

Uu's underground,
where some vegetables grow,
Like the beet, carrot, radish,
and the *poe-tay-toe*.

Vv is for vines.
Whether pumpkin or bean,
They're twisty and twiney
and leafy and green.

Ww's for water—
from can or from hose
Or sometimes from rain
that just comes and goes.

Xx is excitement.
No time to be wasting.
Whatever is ready
is ready for tasting.

Yy is for year,
with winter for sleeping,
Springtime for planting,
fall and summer for reaping.

Zz is for zzzzzzz.

Those are bees on the wing.
Alive in the hive, they'll be
back in the spring.

DO NOT DISTURB UNTIL SPRING